The Christmas Game

Jesse Matz

Copyright © 2024 Jesse Matz

All rights reserved. No part of this book may be reproduced or transmitted in any form or by any means, electronic or mechanical, including photocopying, recording or by any information storage and retrieval system without permission in writing from the publisher.

Luna's Library—Middleton, WI
ISBN: 979-8-218-55452-1
Library of Congress Control Number: 2024924506
Title: *The Christmas Game*
Author: Jesse Matz
Paperback | 2024

Published in the United States by New Book Authors Publishing

Dedication

This book is dedicated to my Family, I Love You! And in memory of my middle school guidance counselor, Agneta Sarinske. Whom helped guide me through some difficult years.

This story is based on true events that occurred in our family home on December 25th 2023

The morning of Christmas all presents unwrapped.
Time for Dad's Christmas game that he carefully mapped.

It was about to be played by a sister and two brothers.
Their stockings were given to them by their Mother.

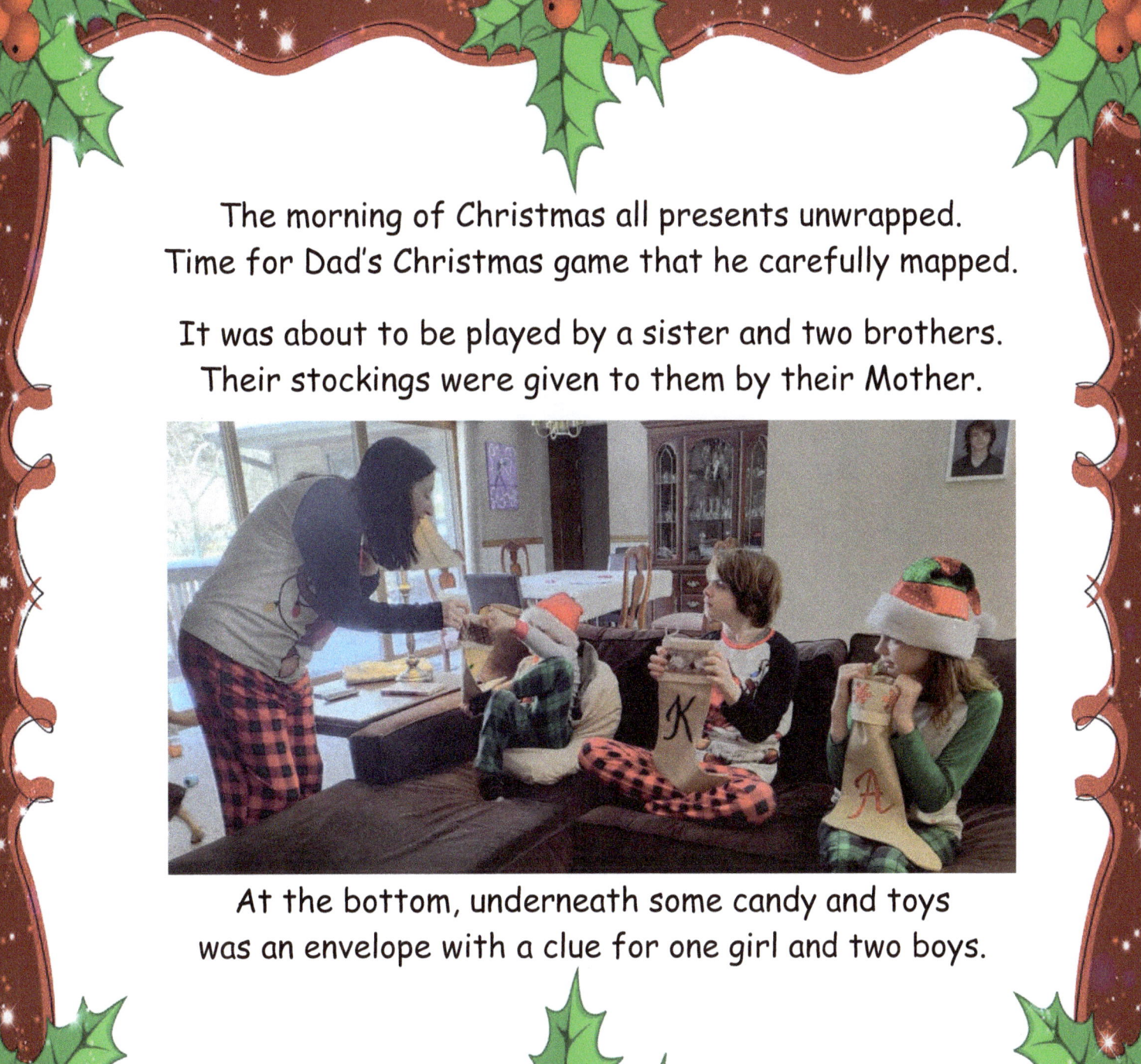

At the bottom, underneath some candy and toys
was an envelope with a clue for one girl and two boys.

We'll start with the oldest
who'd played the game more.
His clues were the hardest
that was for sure.

He opened the envelope and
pulled out the clue
and read the words that
told him what to do!

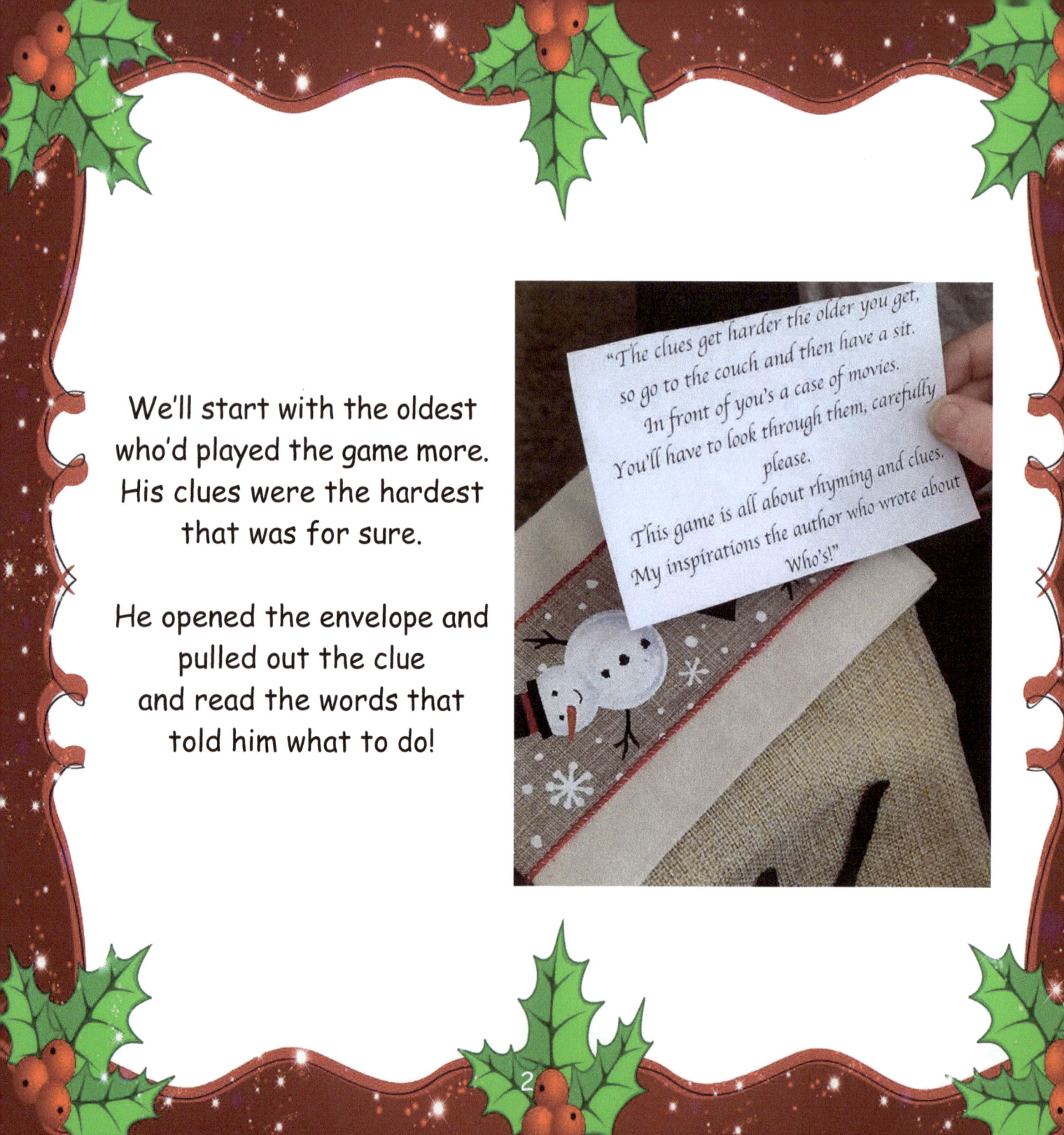

"The clues get harder the older you get,
so go to the couch and then have a sit.
In front of you's a case of movies.
You'll have to look through them, carefully please.
This game is all about rhyming and clues.
My inspirations the author who wrote about Who's!"

So he did exactly what the clue said.
He sat on the couch and there straight ahead,
was the case that was mentioned.
He looked through to see,
where his clue would be found,
behind which kids movie.
He checked behind the one with the green grouch. Instead,
it was behind the one with the elephant. He pulled it out, and then read...

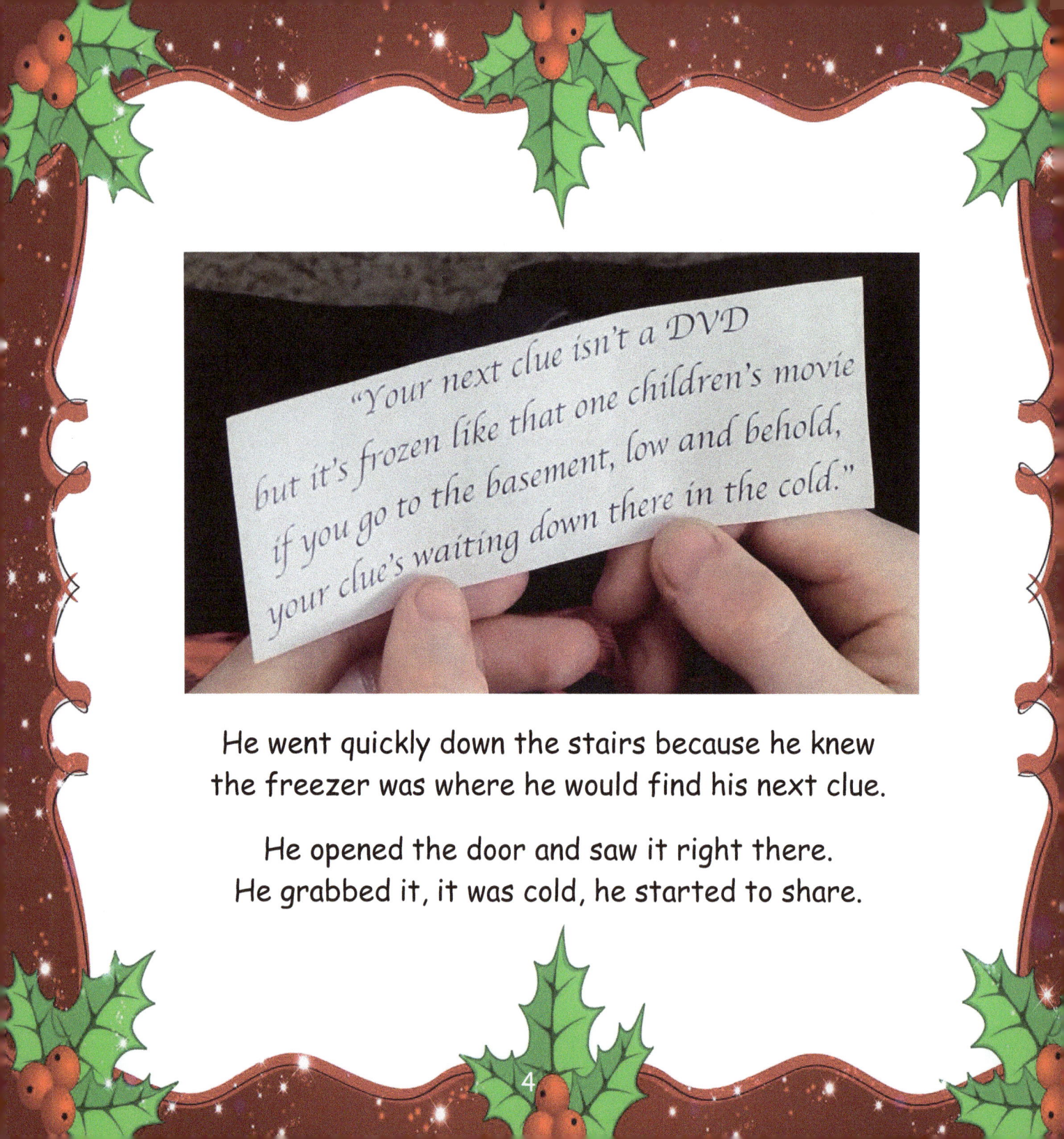

"Your next clue isn't a DVD
but it's frozen like that one children's movie
if you go to the basement, low and behold,
your clue's waiting down there in the cold."

He went quickly down the stairs because he knew
the freezer was where he would find his next clue.

He opened the door and saw it right there.
He grabbed it, it was cold, he started to share.

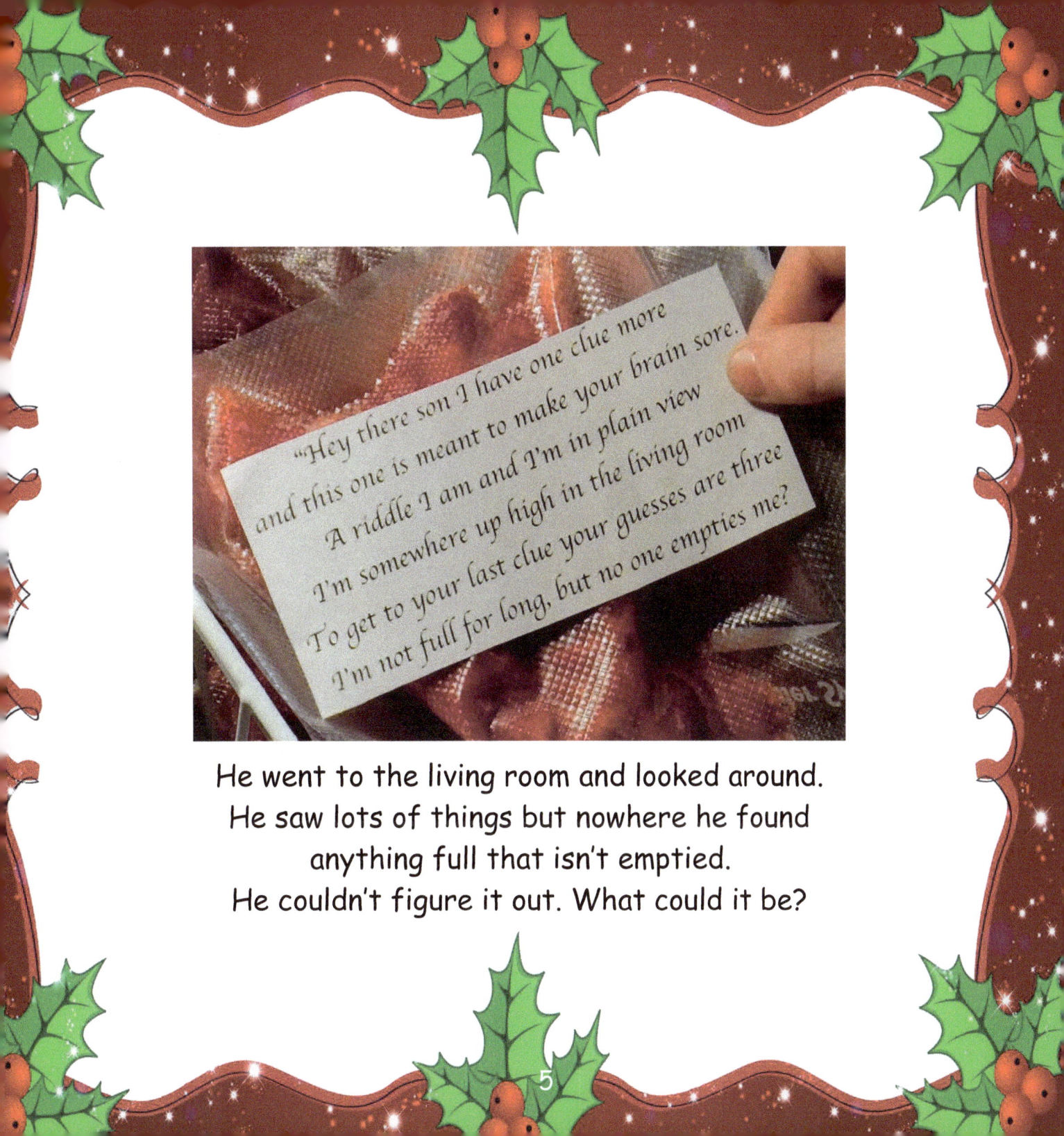

"Hey there son I have one clue more
and this one is meant to make your brain sore.
A riddle I am and I'm in plain view
I'm somewhere up high in the living room
To get to your last clue your guesses are three
I'm not full for long, but no one empties me?

He went to the living room and looked around.
He saw lots of things but nowhere he found
anything full that isn't emptied.
He couldn't figure it out. What could it be?

Then he saw something out of the corner of his eye.
It was a lamp in the shape of the moon in the sky.

The moon's not full for long, and it isn't emptied out.
He lifted up the lamp. "The last clue!" he did shout.

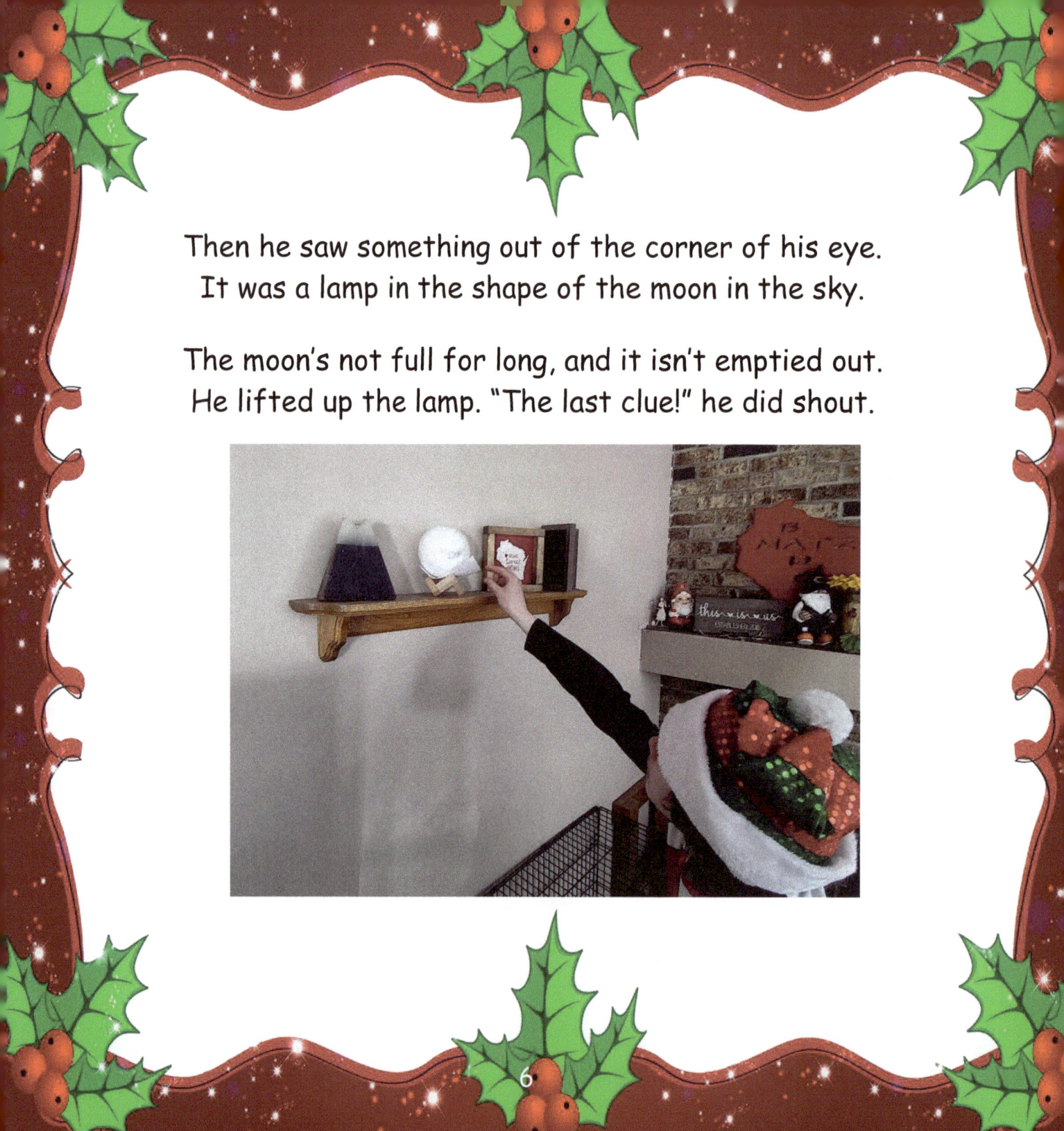

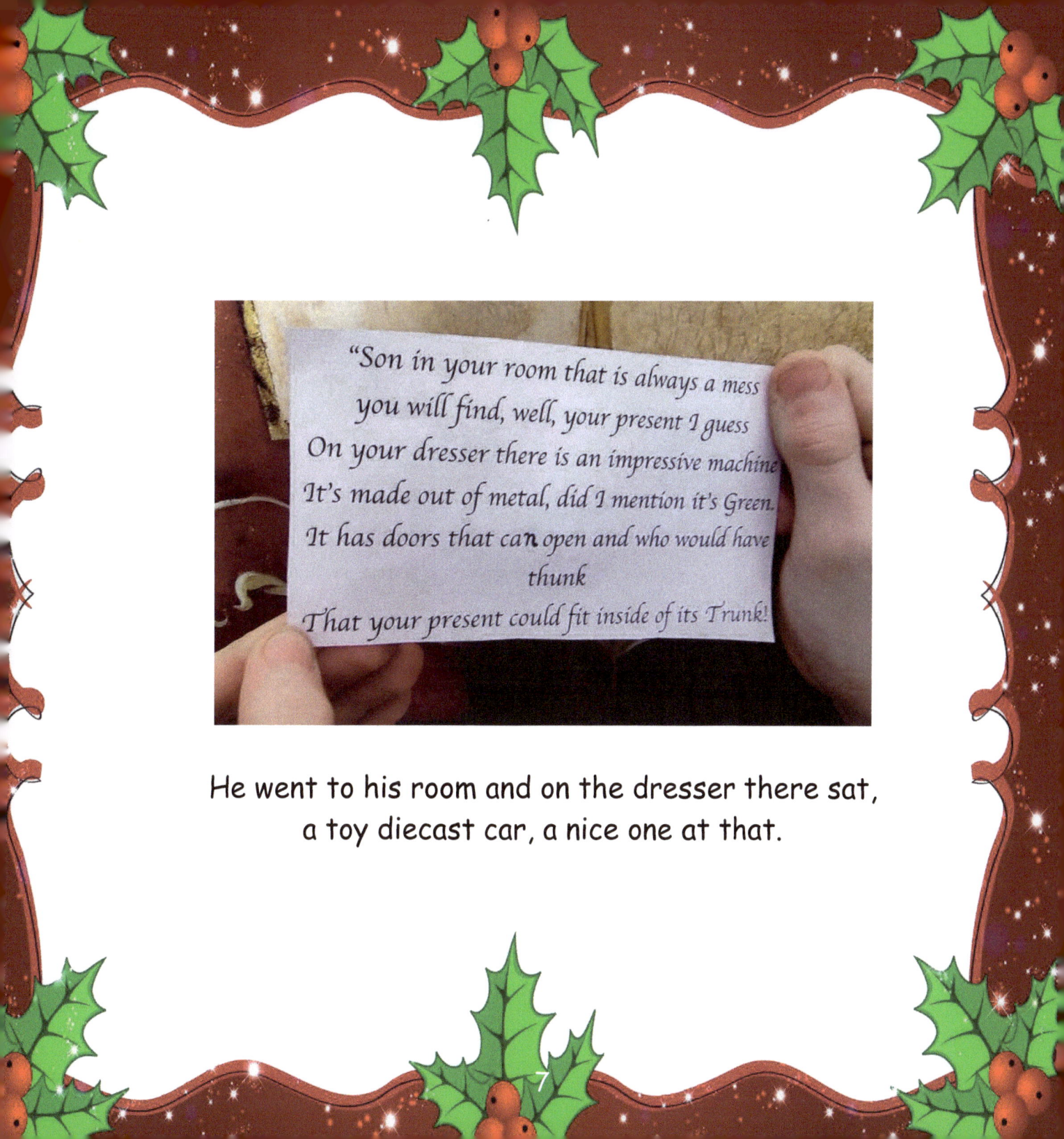

"Son in your room that is always a mess
you will find, well, your present I guess
On your dresser there is an impressive machine
It's made out of metal, did I mention it's Green.
It has doors that can open and who would have thunk
That your present could fit inside of its Trunk!

He went to his room and on the dresser there sat,
a toy diecast car, a nice one at that.

He opened the trunk and what did he see?
A coin made of silver, a Lady Liberty!

Now it was time for the sweet little girl
to open her card and give it a whirl...

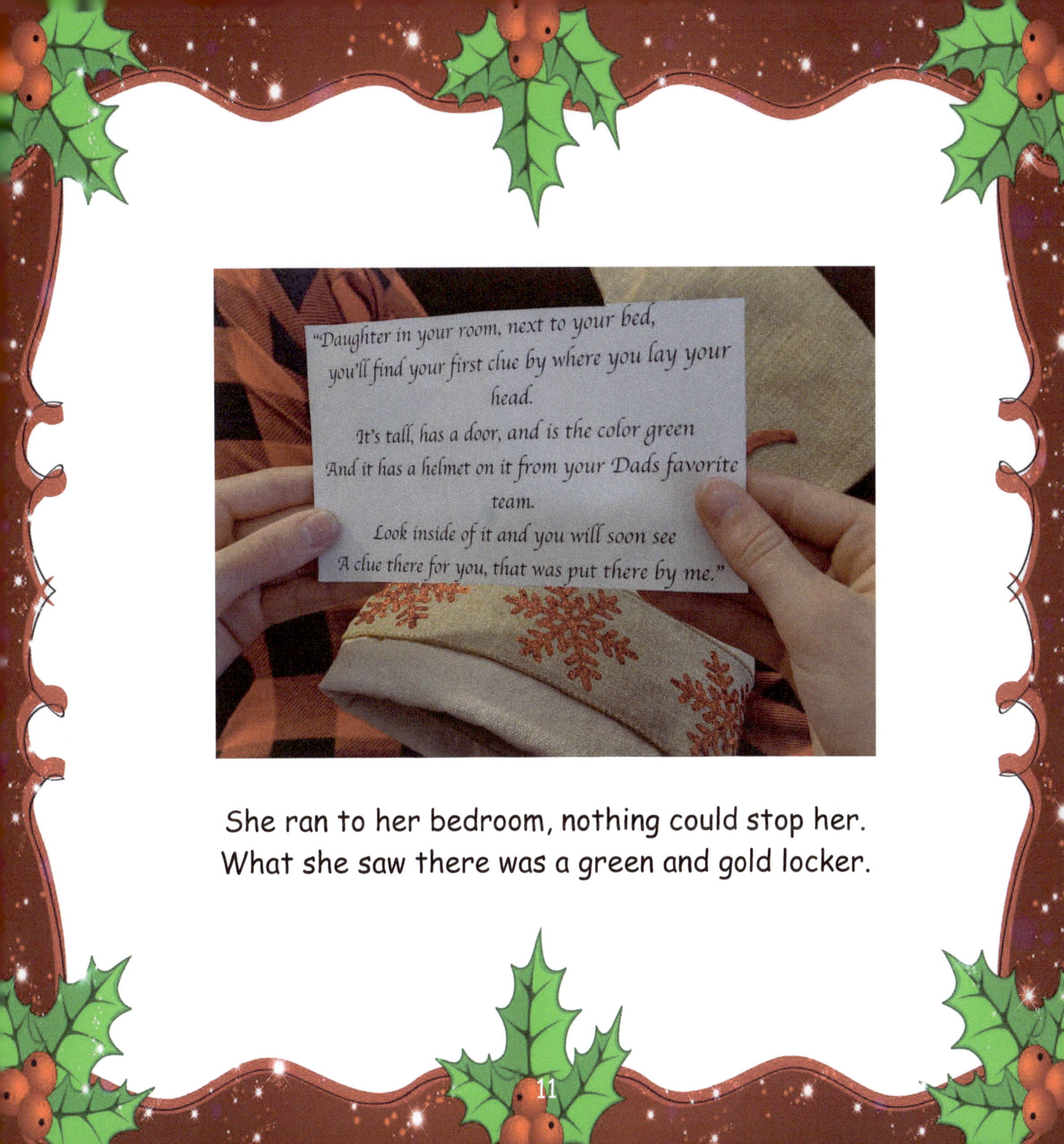

"Daughter in your room, next to your bed,
you'll find your first clue by where you lay your head.
It's tall, has a door, and is the color green
And it has a helmet on it from your Dads favorite team.
Look inside of it and you will soon see
A clue there for you, that was put there by me."

She ran to her bedroom, nothing could stop her.
What she saw there was a green and gold locker.

She opened it up and what did she find?
It was clue number two, so she read the next rhyme.

> "This clue is hidden in something from your Christmas past.
> It is inside a gift from the year of last
> Since then a whole lot of your time was spent
> Hiding and playing inside of your tent."

She ran down the stairs just as fast as she could,
to find her next clue, and I knew that she would.

She went in her tent and looked all around.
In the top, in the peak, was where it was found.

She grabbed it and then she knew just what to do.
She opened it up and she read her next clue.

"Did you know your Dad was locally known.
For making good food like he does, for you, at home.
He did it with proficiency, skill, and tact.
If you don't believe me? Take a look at his plaque."

She went to the kitchen and on the wall there hung,
a plaque with her dad's name for a competition he won.

Under a corner she found her last rhyme.
She read with excitement, because it was present time!

"Darling the whole time you opened your gifts up
This present was inches away from you... "Hold up!
How is that possible?' you might say.
"That my present was only a few inches away."
Well not only was it in the same room as you,
It was also directly underneath of you too!"

She walked to where she was when she opened her gifts.
A love seat was there, so she started to lift.

Underneath it she saw a box wrapped with a bow.
Inside it was a Santa's Elf plushie, wouldn't you know.

There was only one kiddo left to play.
The youngest of three, and it was his special day
because this would be the very first time
he would play his dad's Christmas game of rhyme.

He couldn't read the clues because he was only three.
How would he find his gift? Keep reading and you will see...

The kids all knew where there was such a thing.
A tree that did dance and also did sing.

It was down in the basement standing on a shelf.
They saw a piece of paper sticking out of its mouth.

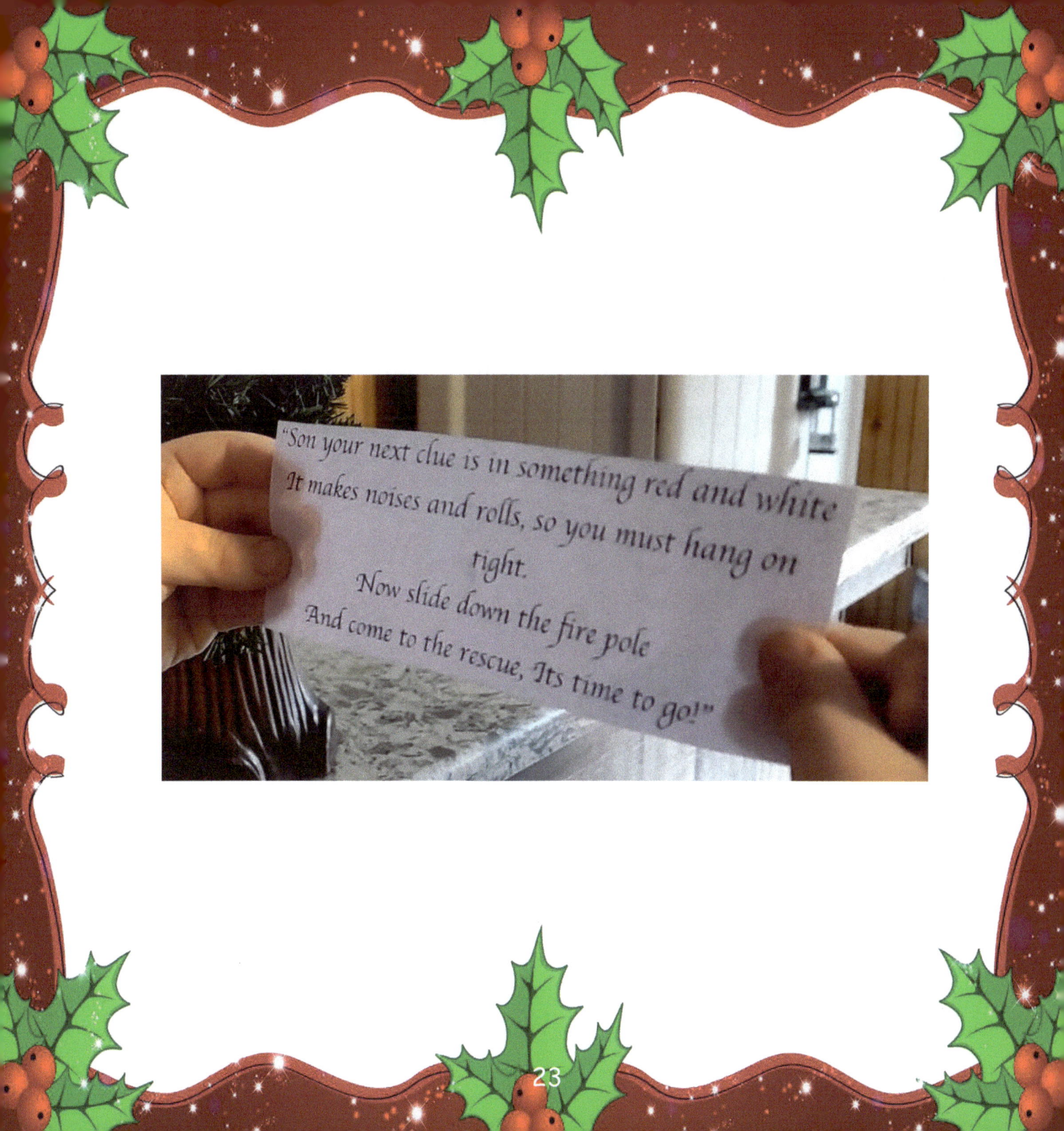

In the living room there was a firetruck toy.
It had a horn and a siren and had brought him much joy.

It also had a compartment under the seat.
That was where he found a folded-up paper sheet.

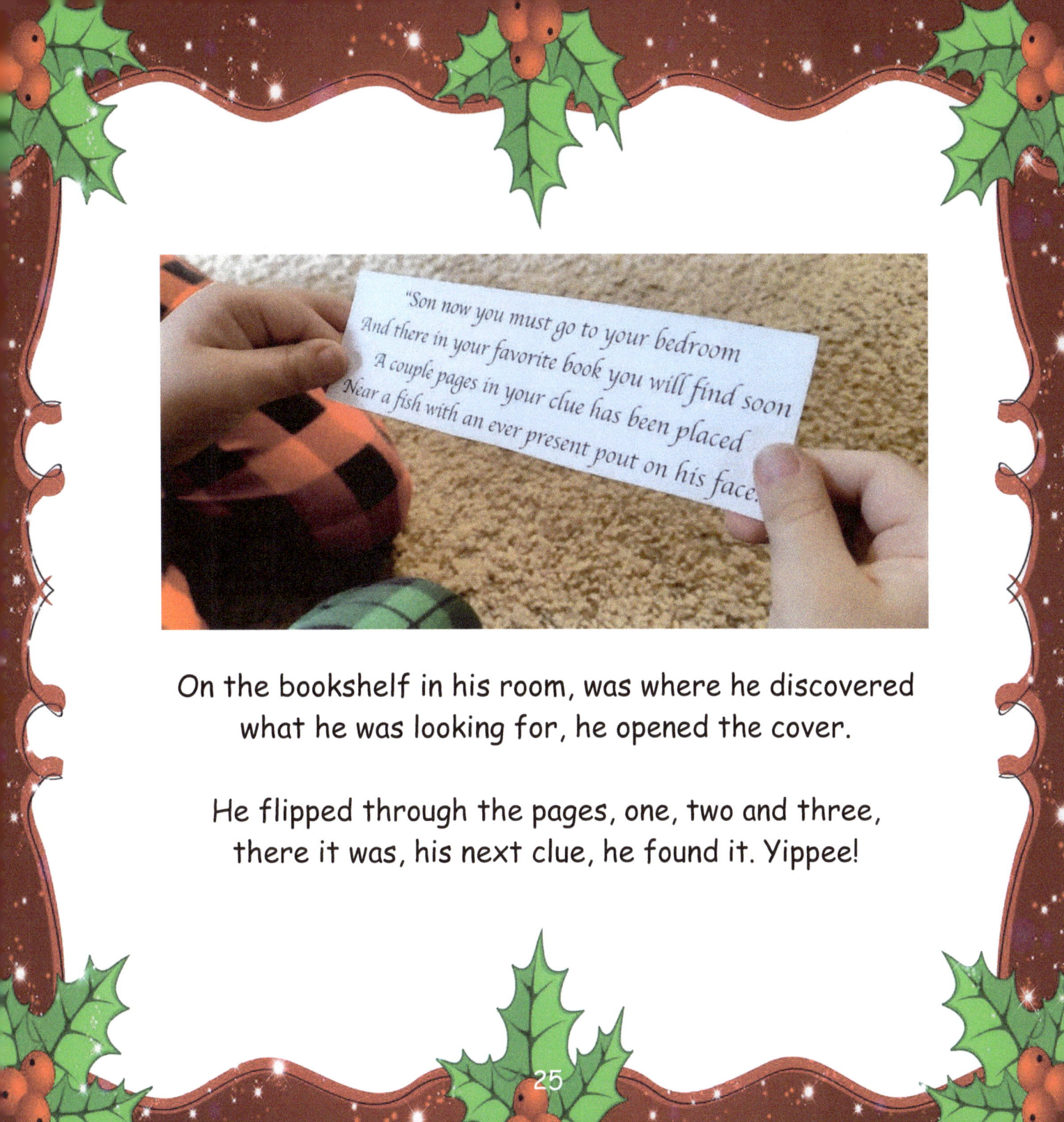

On the bookshelf in his room, was where he discovered what he was looking for, he opened the cover.

He flipped through the pages, one, two and three, there it was, his next clue, he found it. Yippee!

He ran to the closet and opened the door.
His present was sitting right there on the floor.

He took it out and then he shut the door with a smack.

Then he opened up his brand new racecar track!

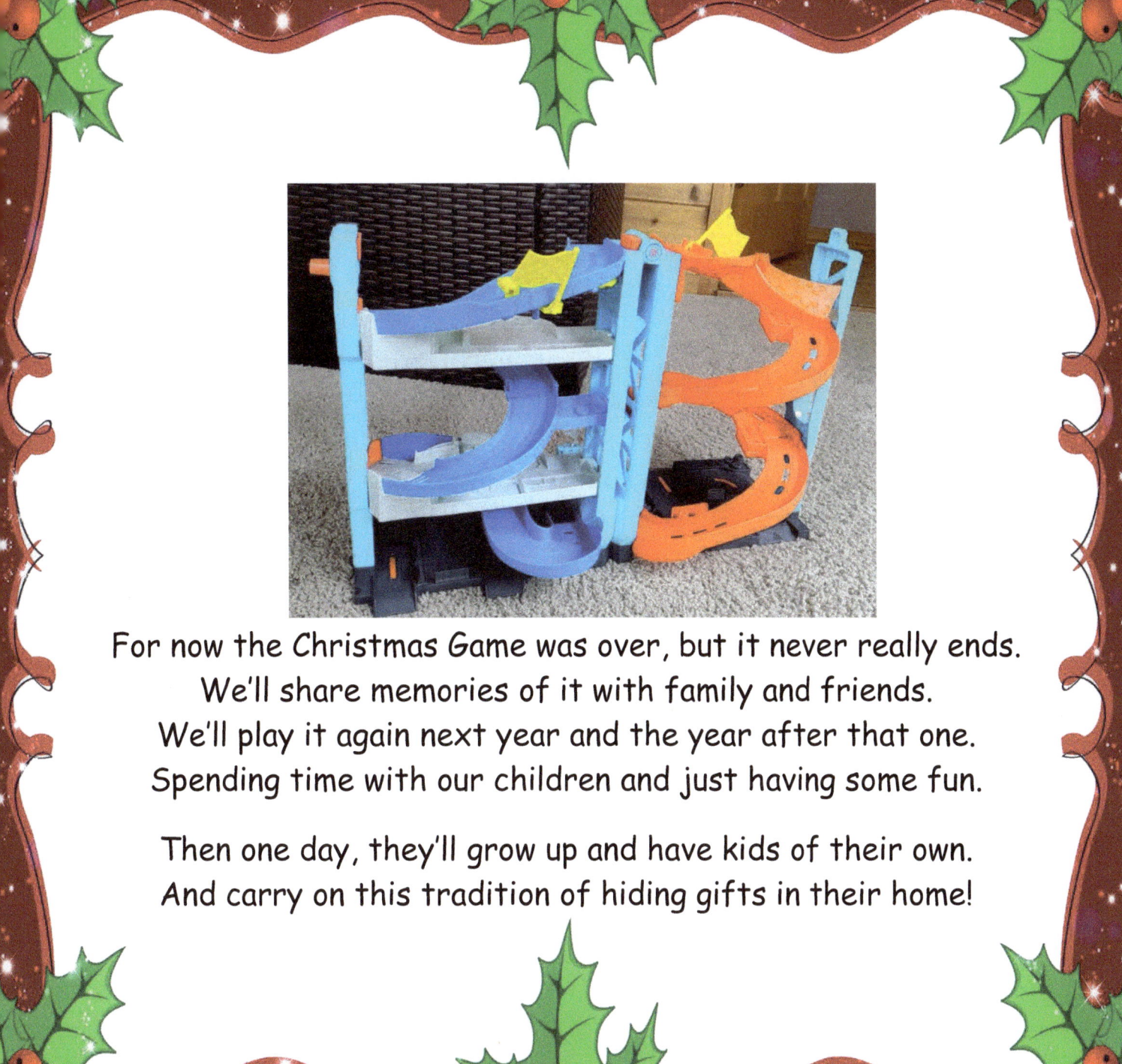

For now the Christmas Game was over, but it never really ends.
We'll share memories of it with family and friends.
We'll play it again next year and the year after that one.
Spending time with our children and just having some fun.

Then one day, they'll grow up and have kids of their own.
And carry on this tradition of hiding gifts in their home!

To everyone out there, here's my challenge to you.
Play this game at Christmas or create one that's new.

It's not just about the presents or the give and take.
It's about spending time with our family, and the memories we make.

Merry Christmas from my family to yours!!

The End

About the Author

Jesse Matz is a husband and a proud father of three wonderfully unique children. He grew up in the small town of Prairie Du Sac, Wisconsin with his parents and two older sisters. He is a renowned Chef in the Madison area where he has been featured in newspapers, magazines, and has won local cooking competitions, such as Madison Food and Wine shows Dueling Chef's. Jesse and his family love the holidays and their traditions. Which include picking cherries every July in Door County, Decorating their home, inside and out, every Halloween. Picking out, and cutting down, their Christmas tree every Thanksgiving. And of course playing The Christmas Game every Christmas morning.

www.ingramcontent.com/pod-product-compliance
Lightning Source LLC
LaVergne TN
LVHW072130060526
838201LV00071B/5003